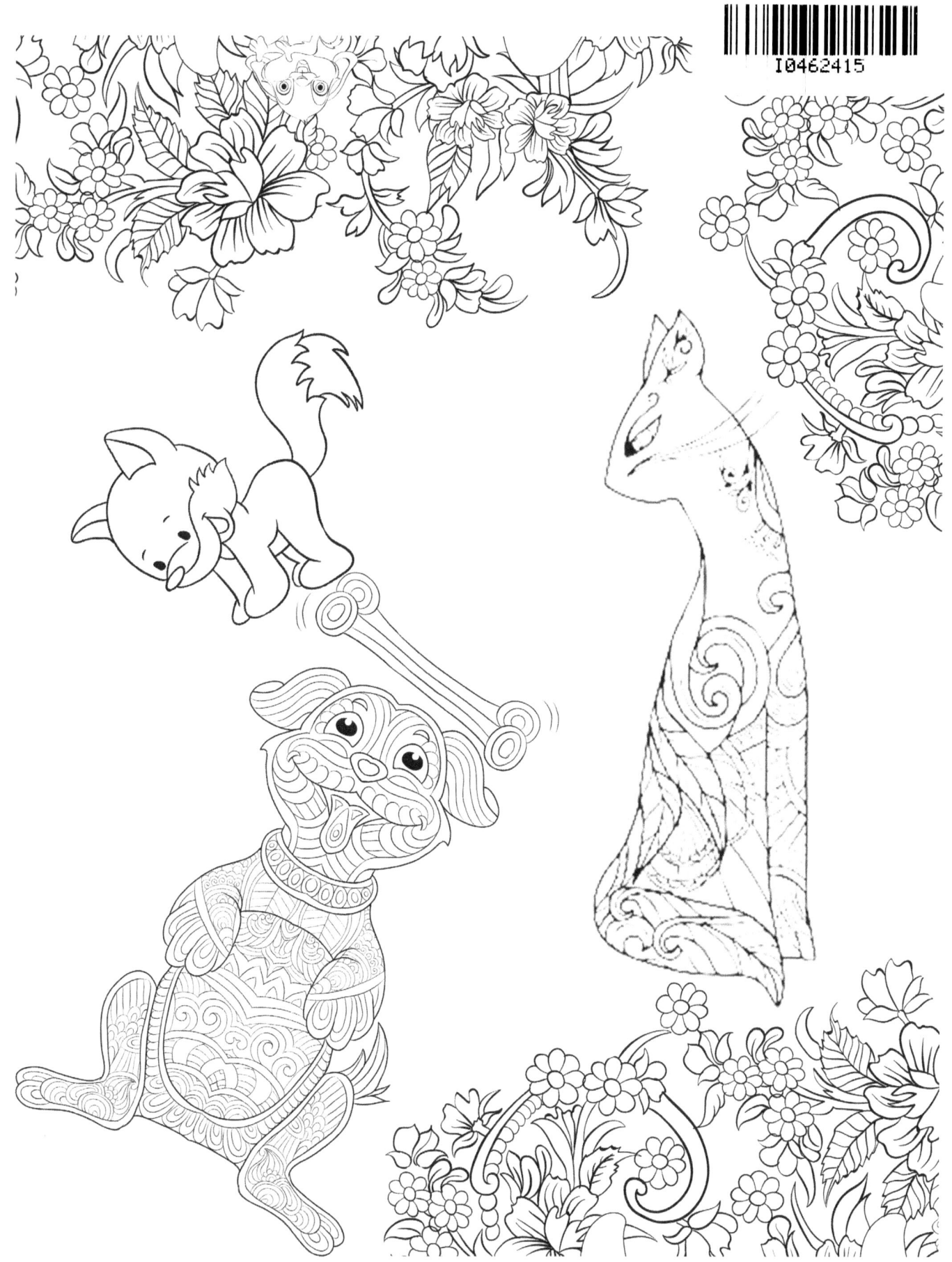

My husband said it was him or the cat... I miss him sometimes.

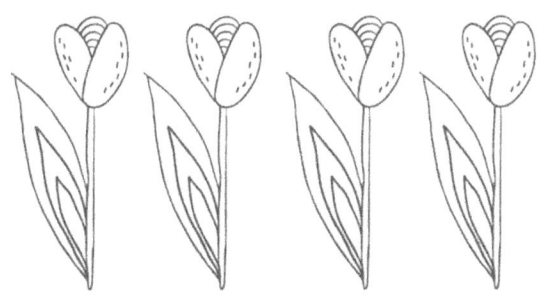

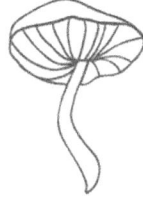

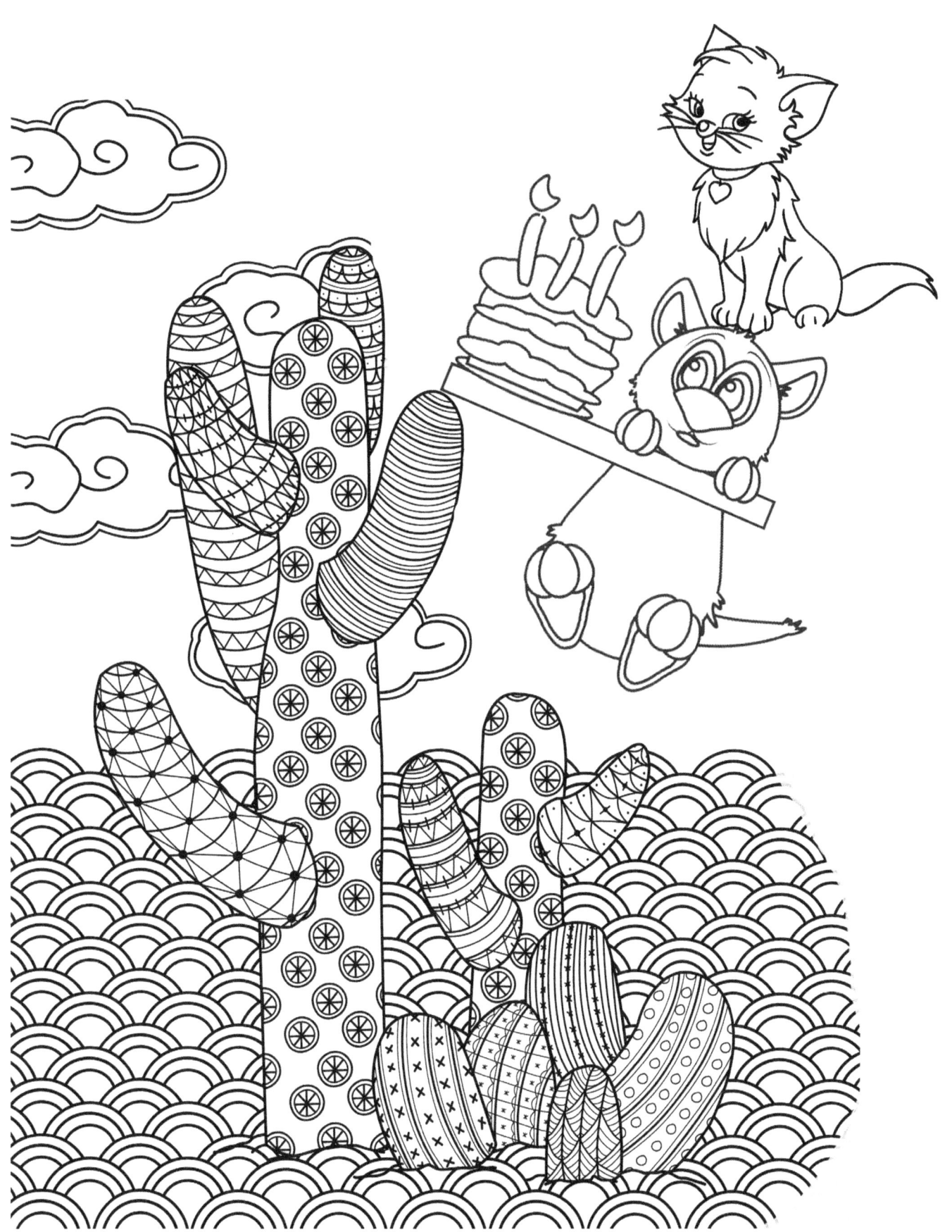

There is no snooze button on a cat who wants breakfast

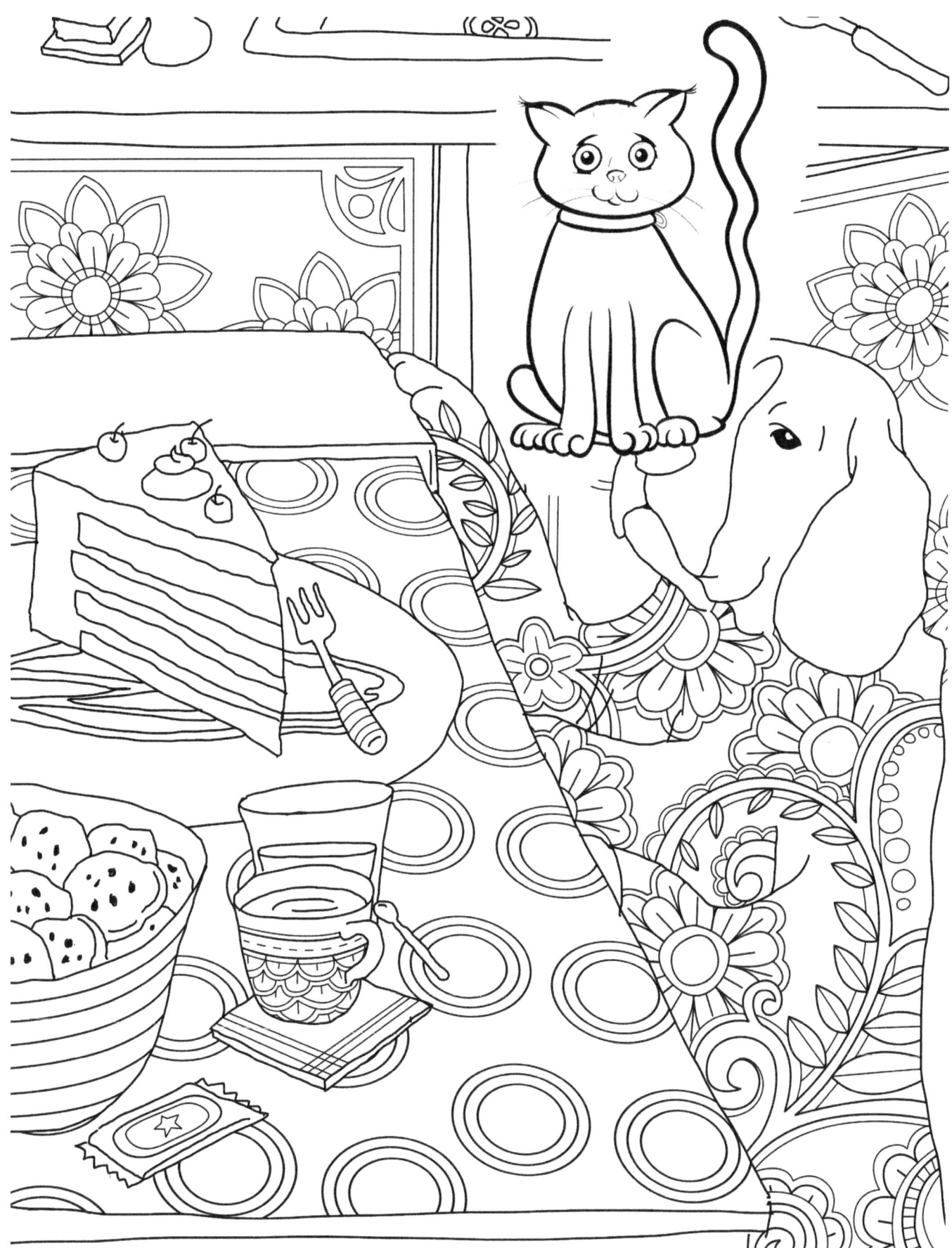

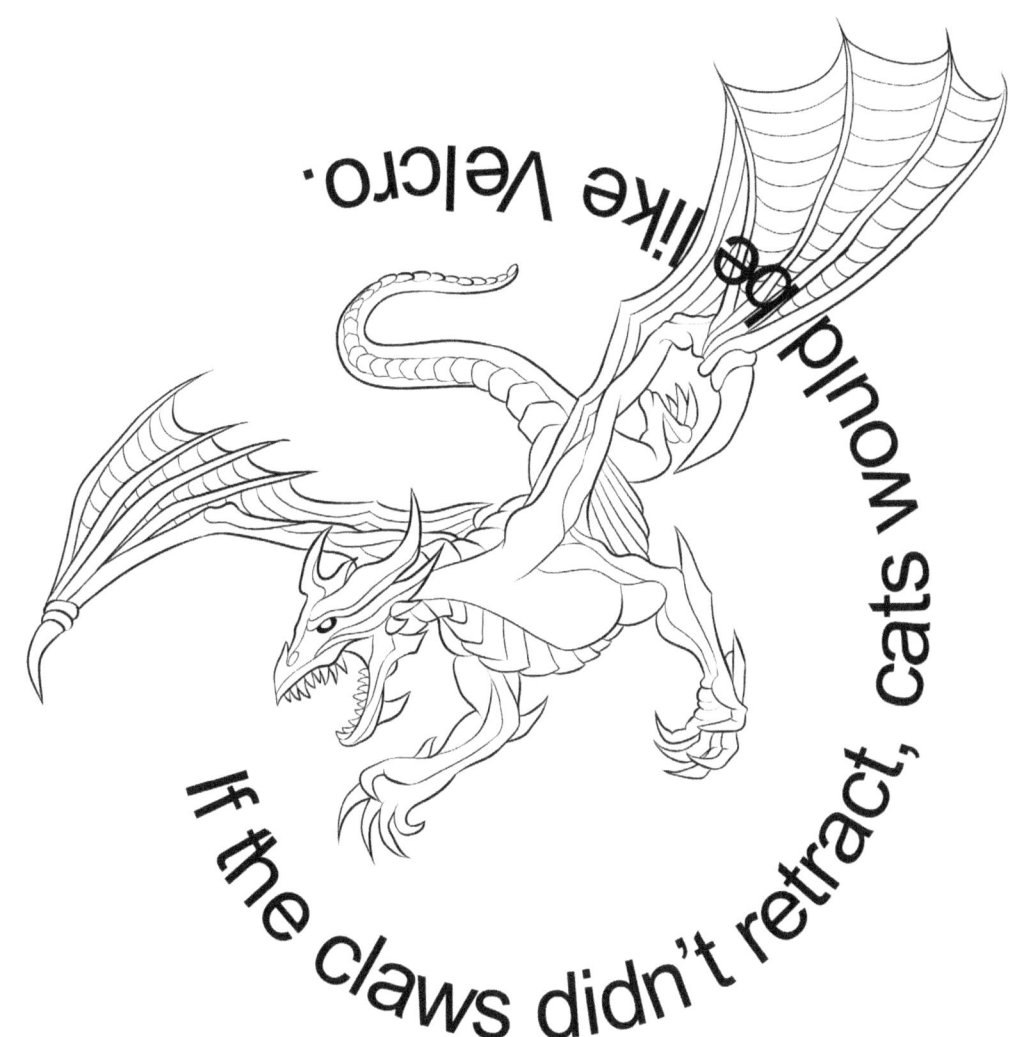

If the claws didn't retract, cats would be like Velcro.

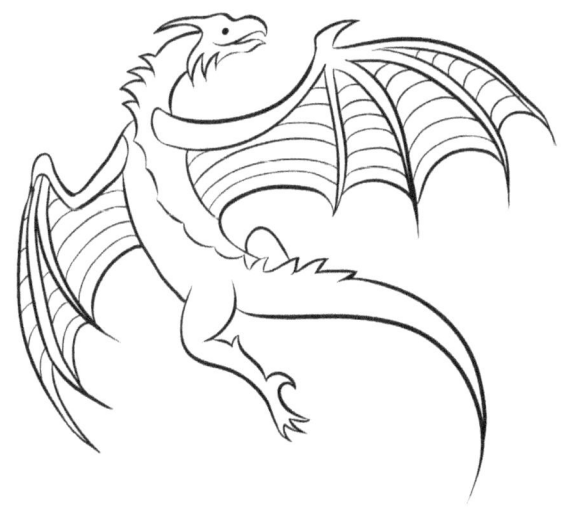

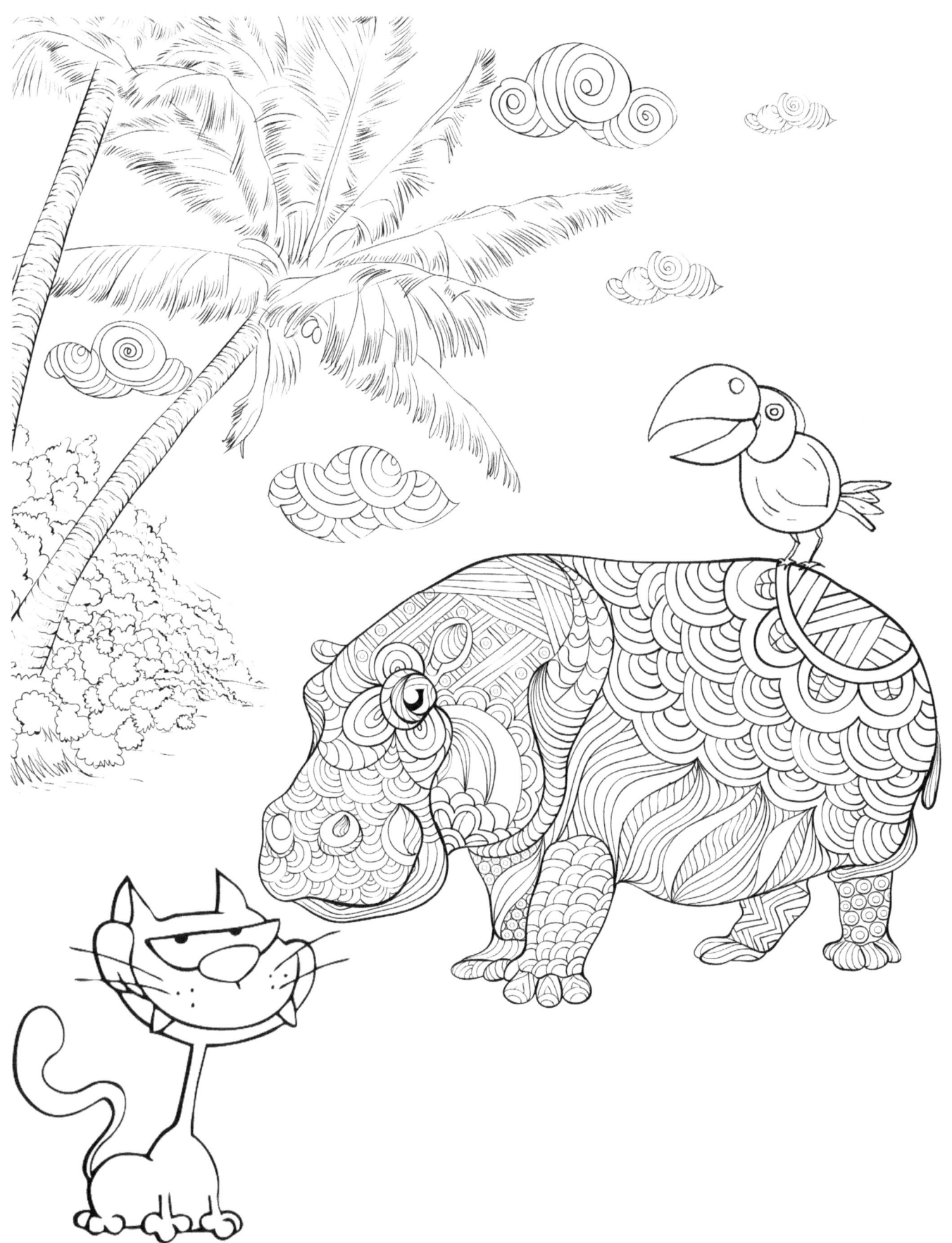

Most beds sleep up to six cats. Ten cats without the owner.

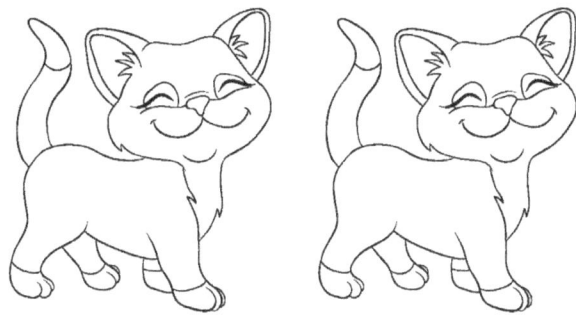

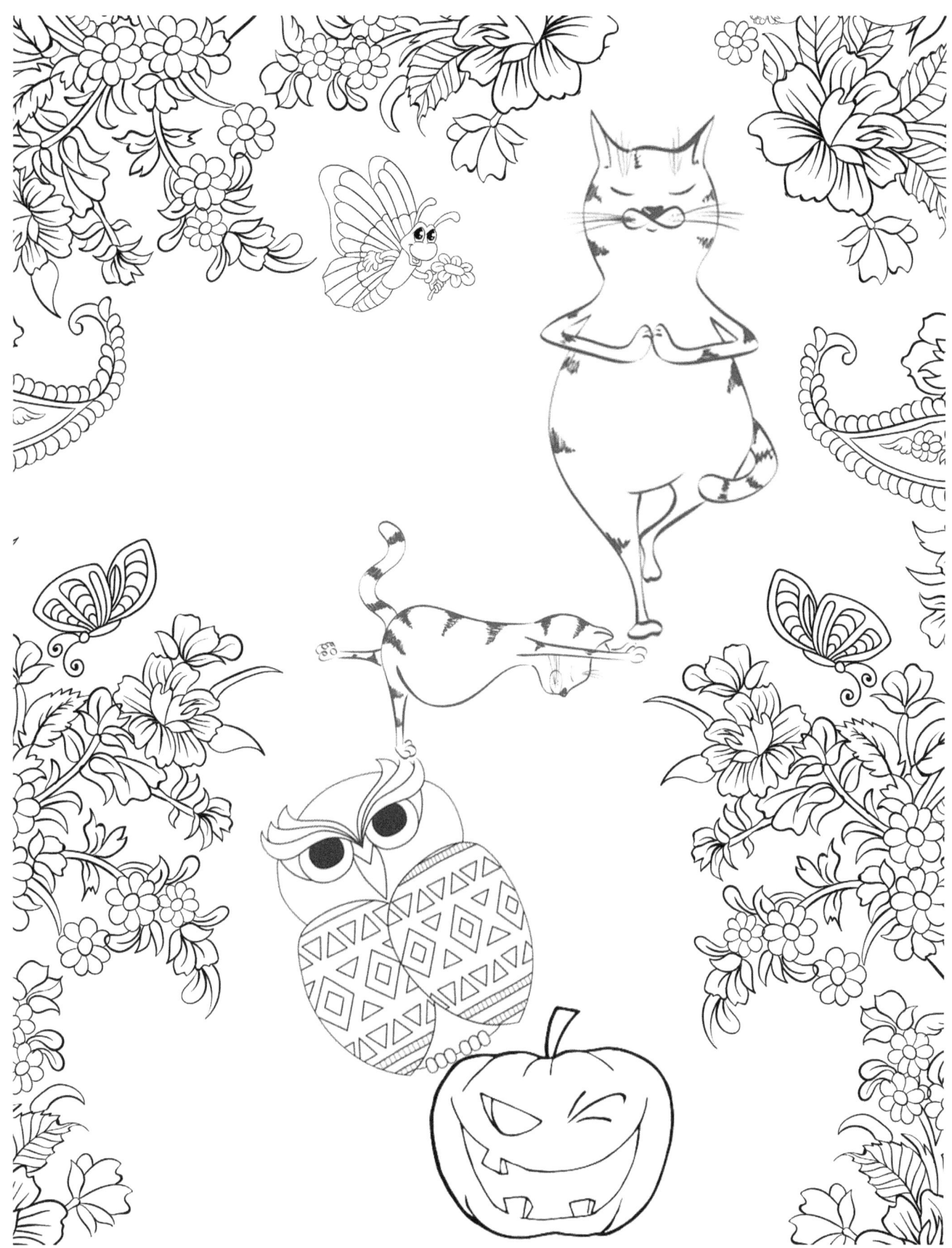

Way down deep, we're all motivated by the same urges. Cats have the courage to live by the.

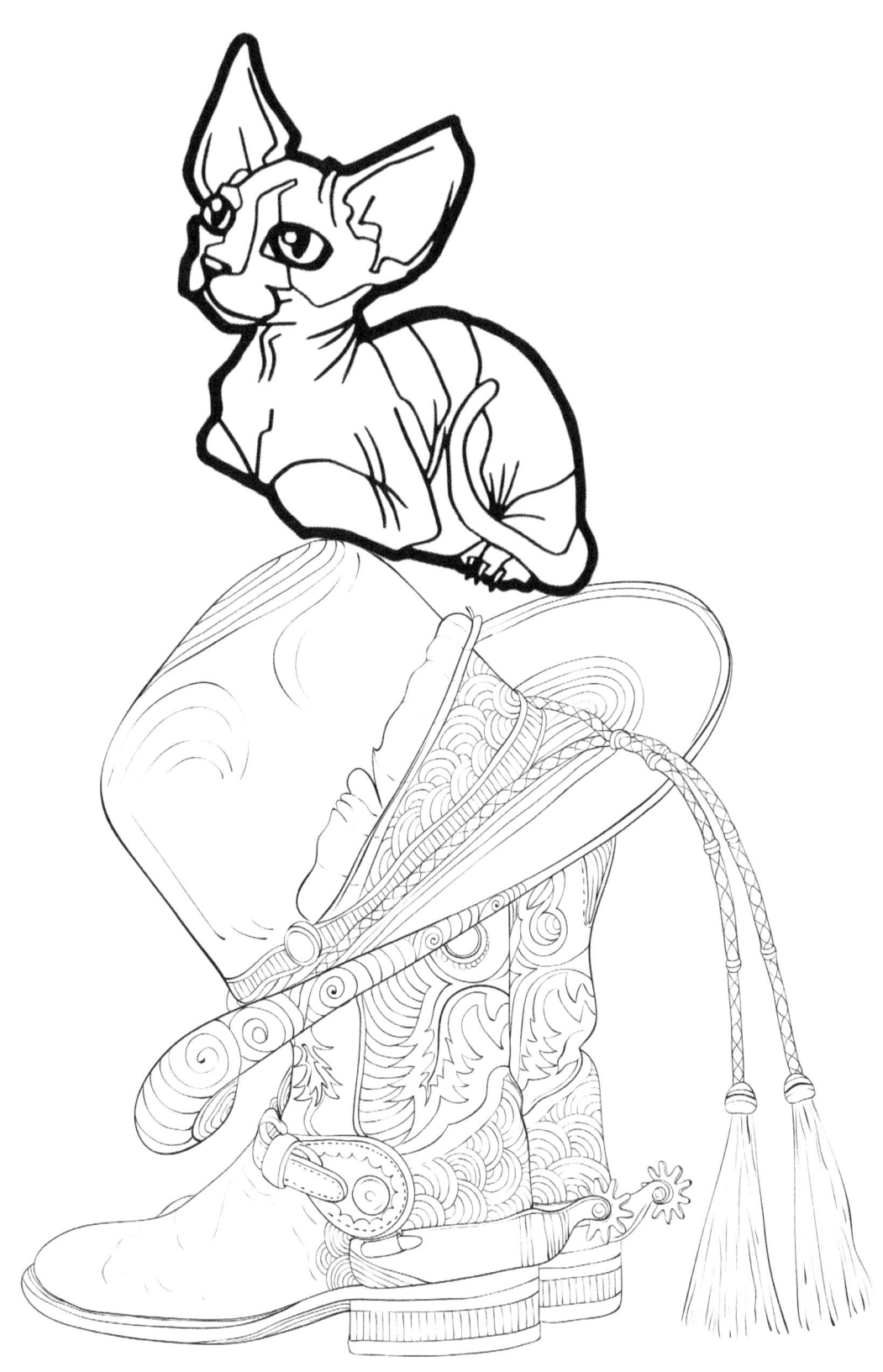

People that hate cats will come back as mice in their next life.

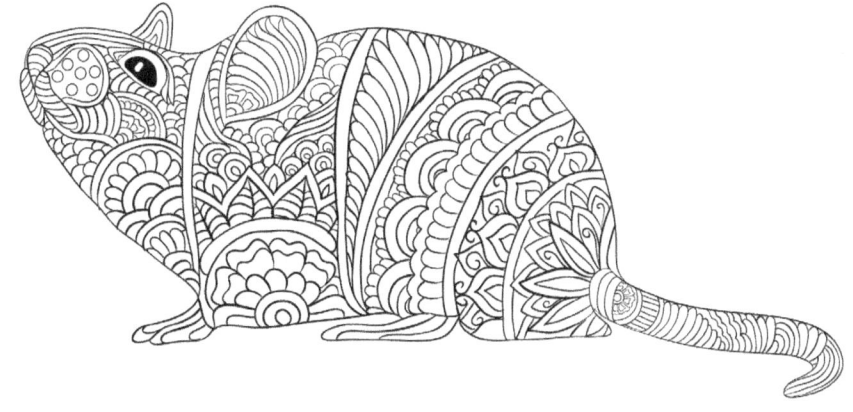

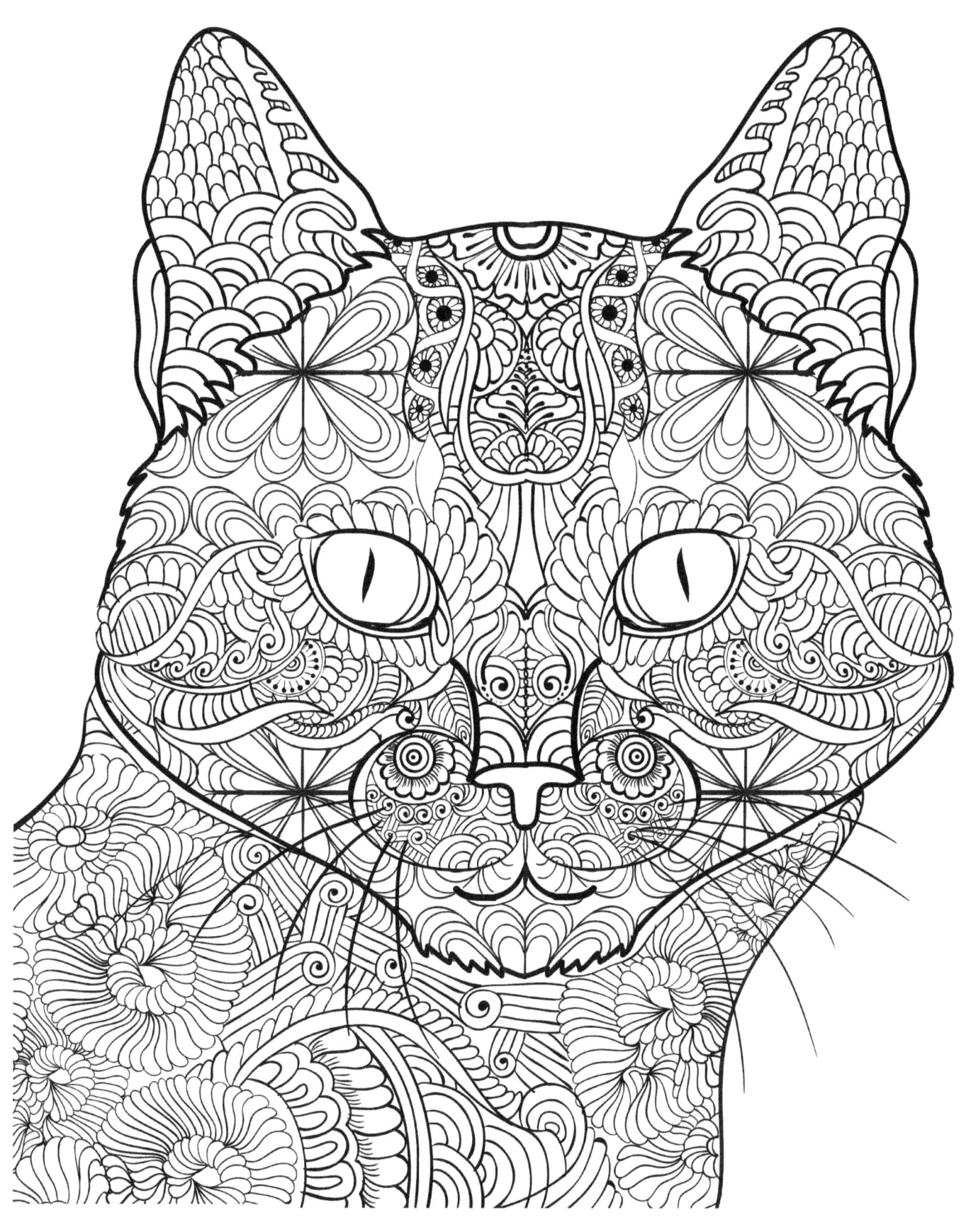

If a dog jumps in your lap, it is because he is fond of you; but if a cat does the same thing, it is because your lap is warmer.

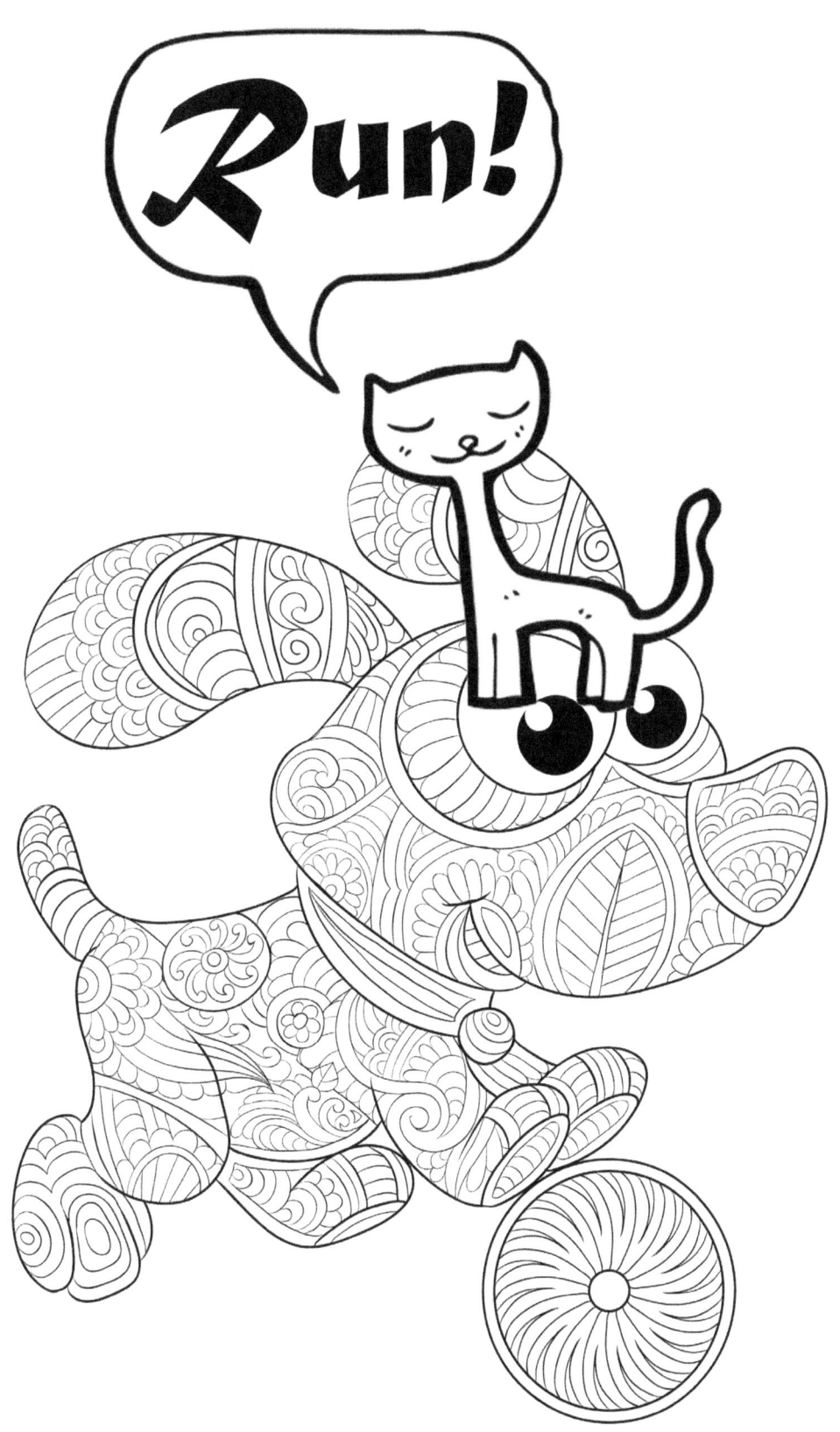

THE WISDOM OF CATS IS INFINITELY SUPERIOR. I HAVE STUDIED MANY PHILOSOPHERS AND MANY CATS. THE WISDOM OF CATS IS INFINITELY SUPERIOR.

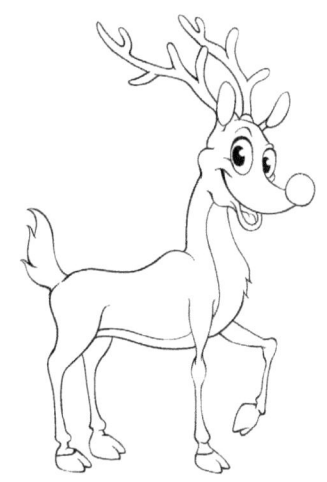

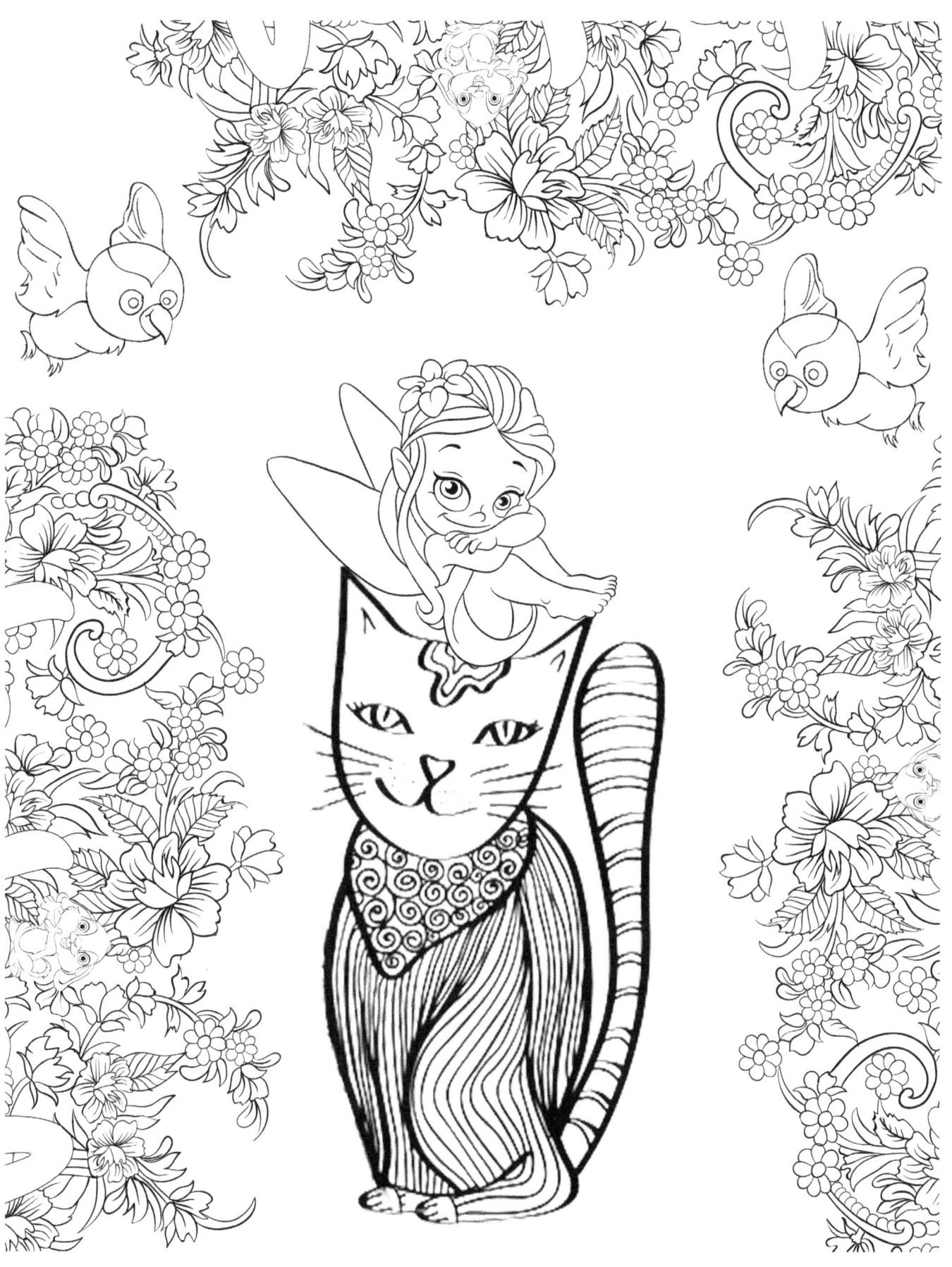

In nine lifetimes, you'll never know as much about your cat as your cat knows about you.

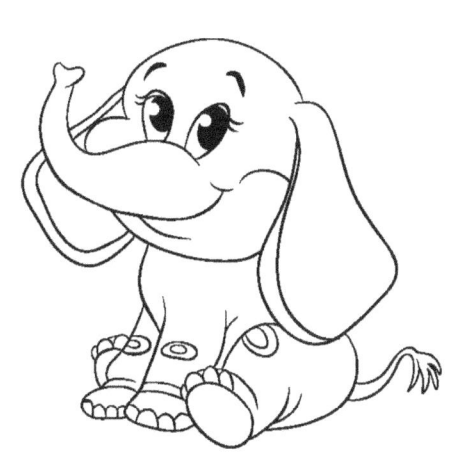

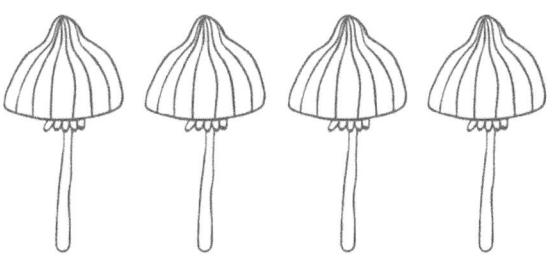

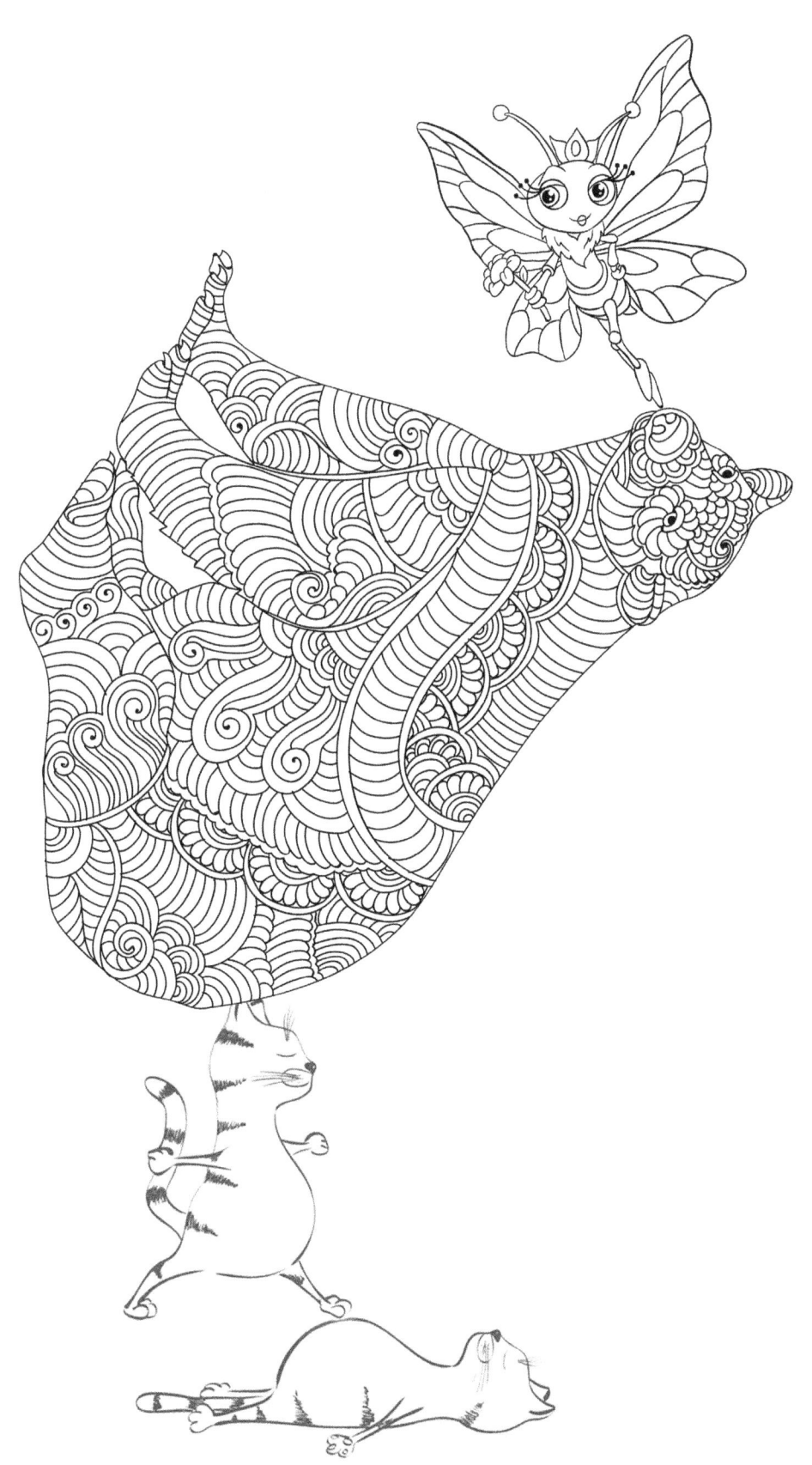

Never try to out stubborn a cat... or two.

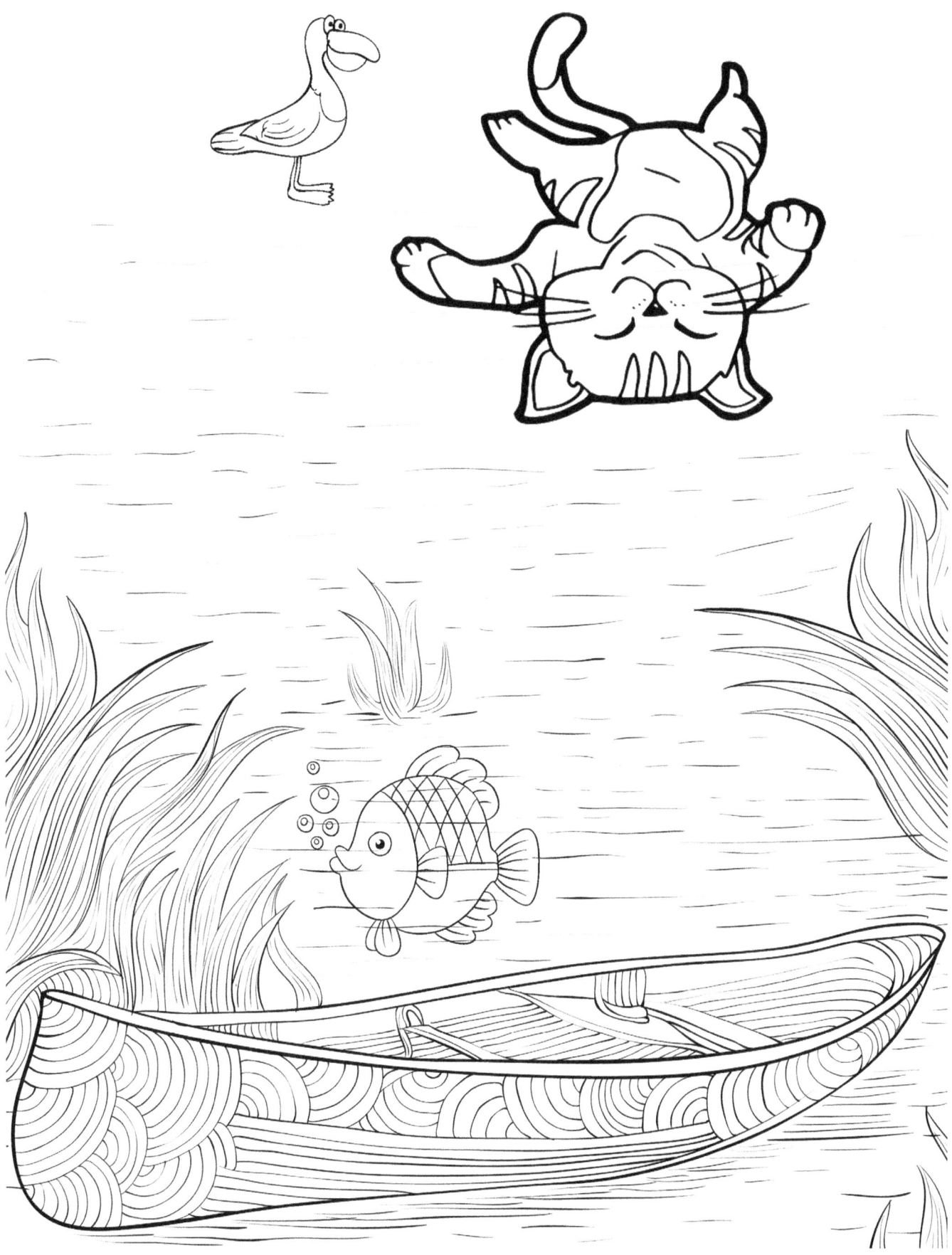

In ancient times cats were worshipped as gods; they have no forgotten this.

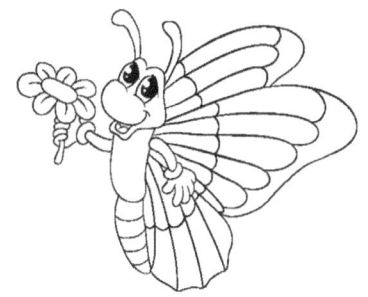

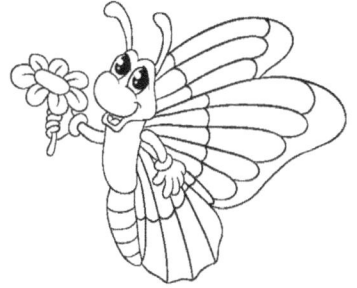

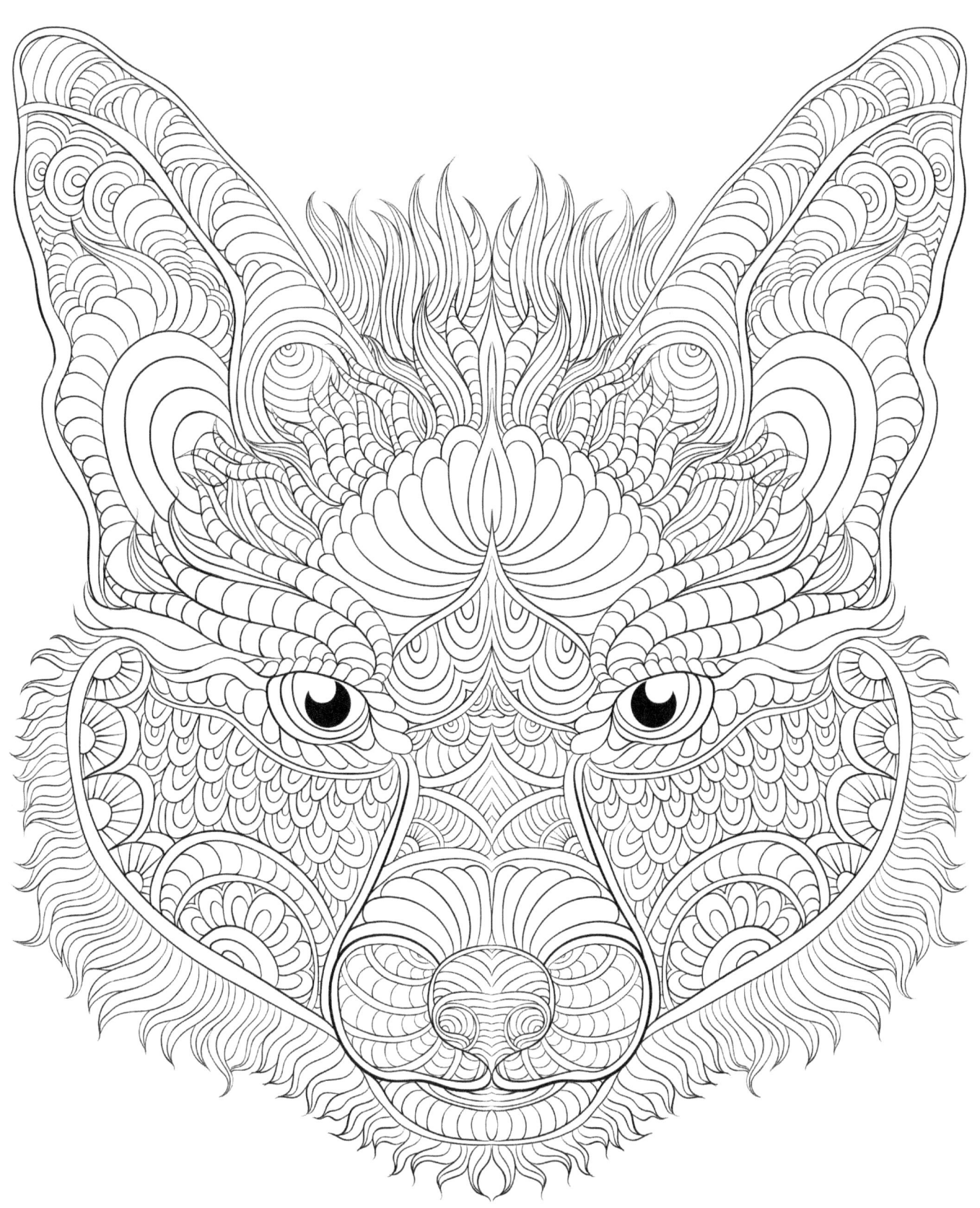

Cats can work out mathematically the exact place to sit that will cause the most inconvenience.

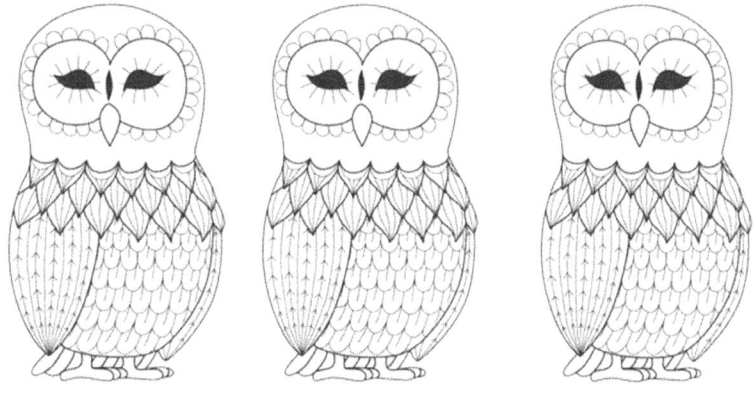

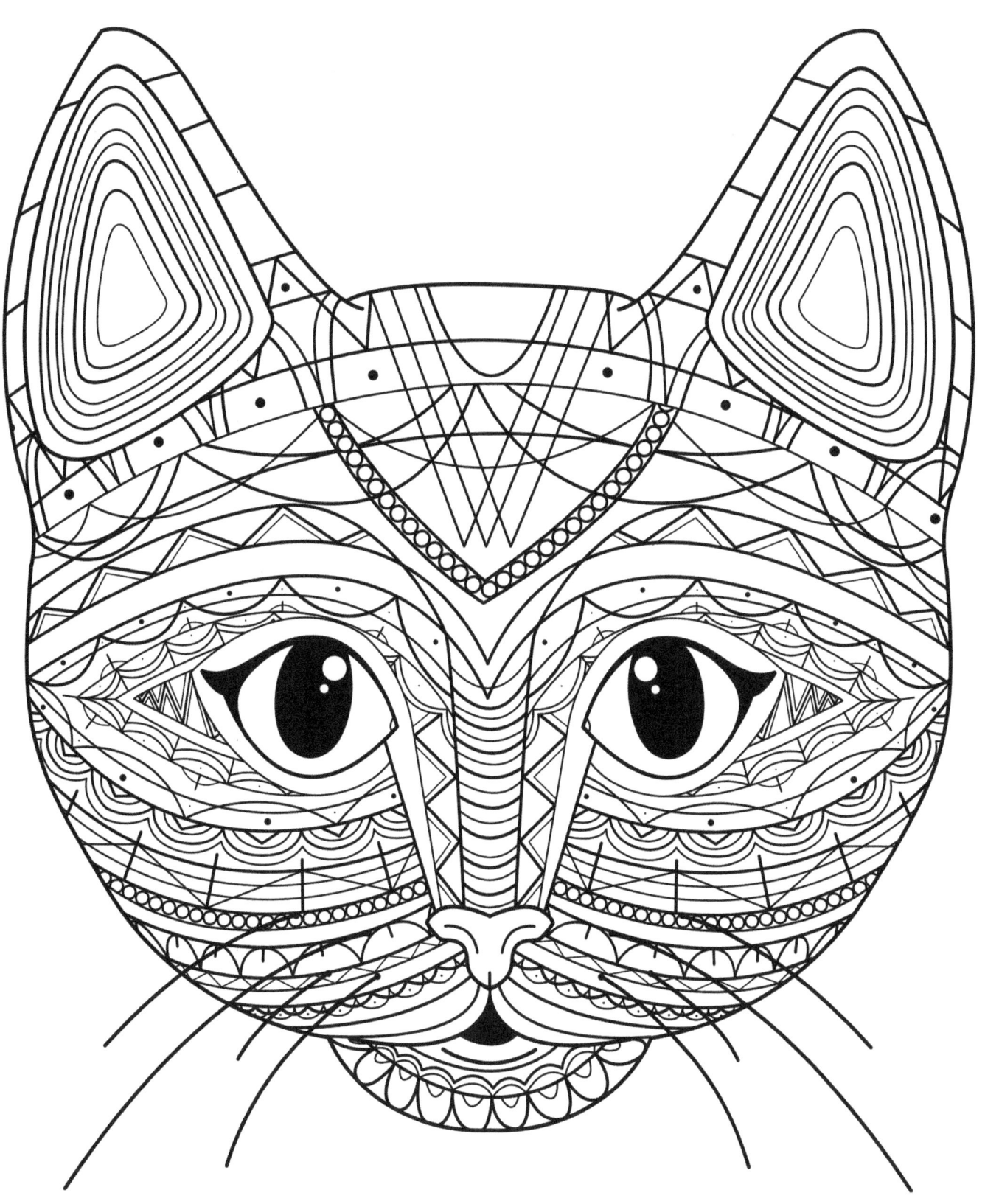

A cat is there when you call her – if she doesn't have something better to do.

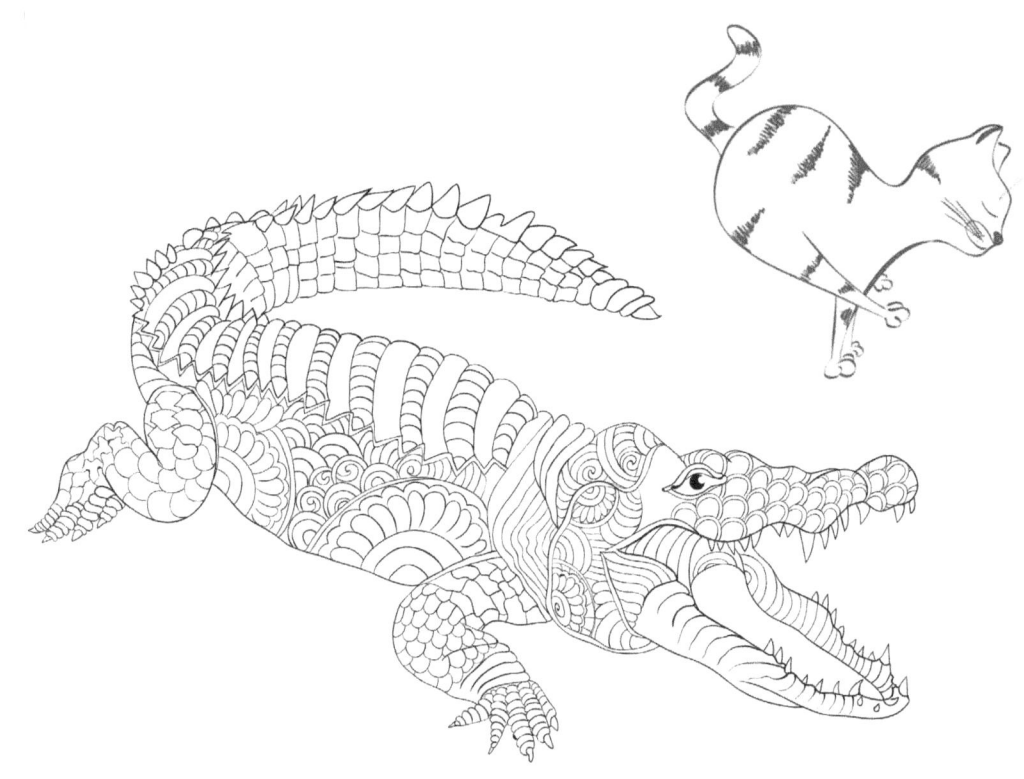

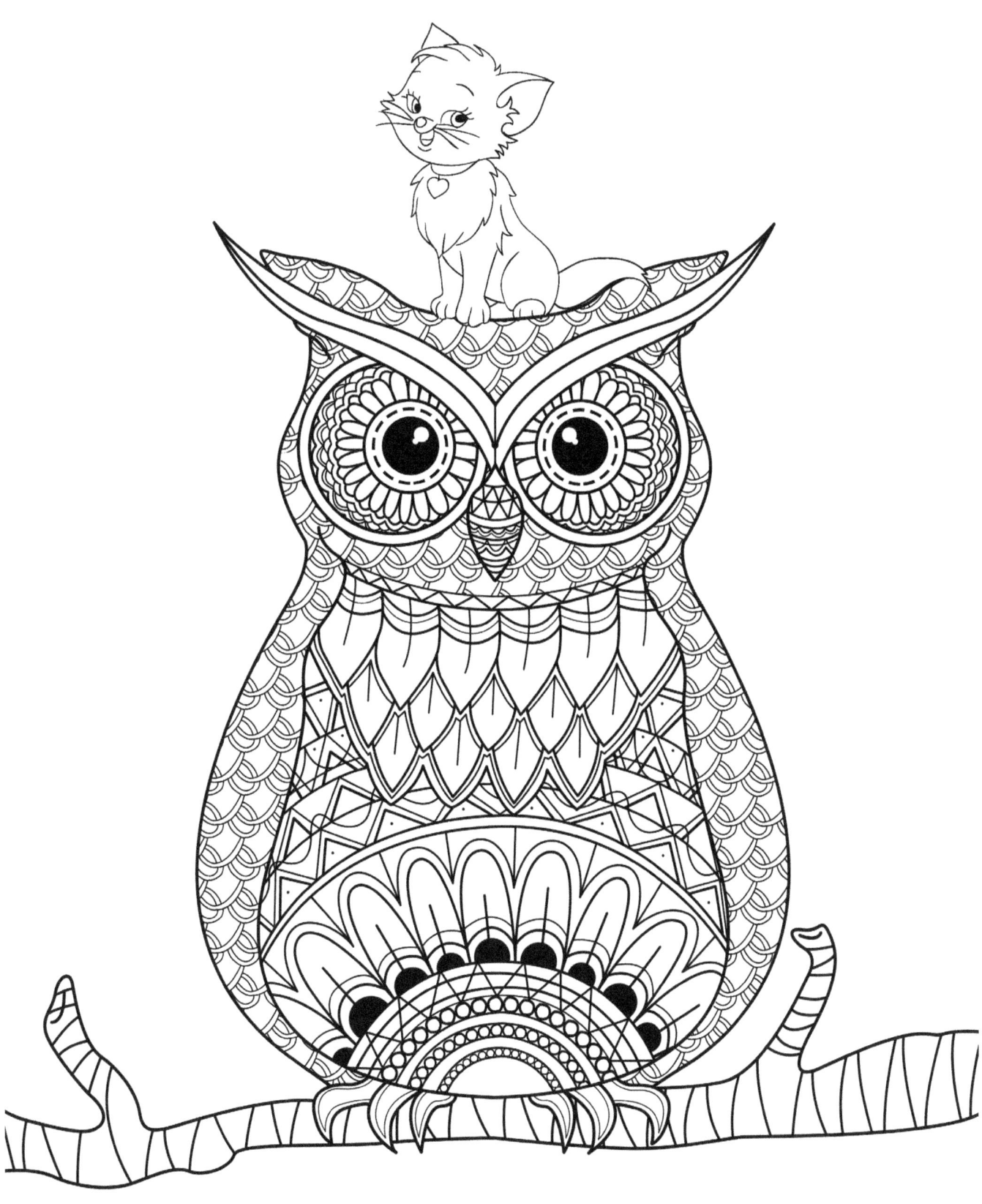

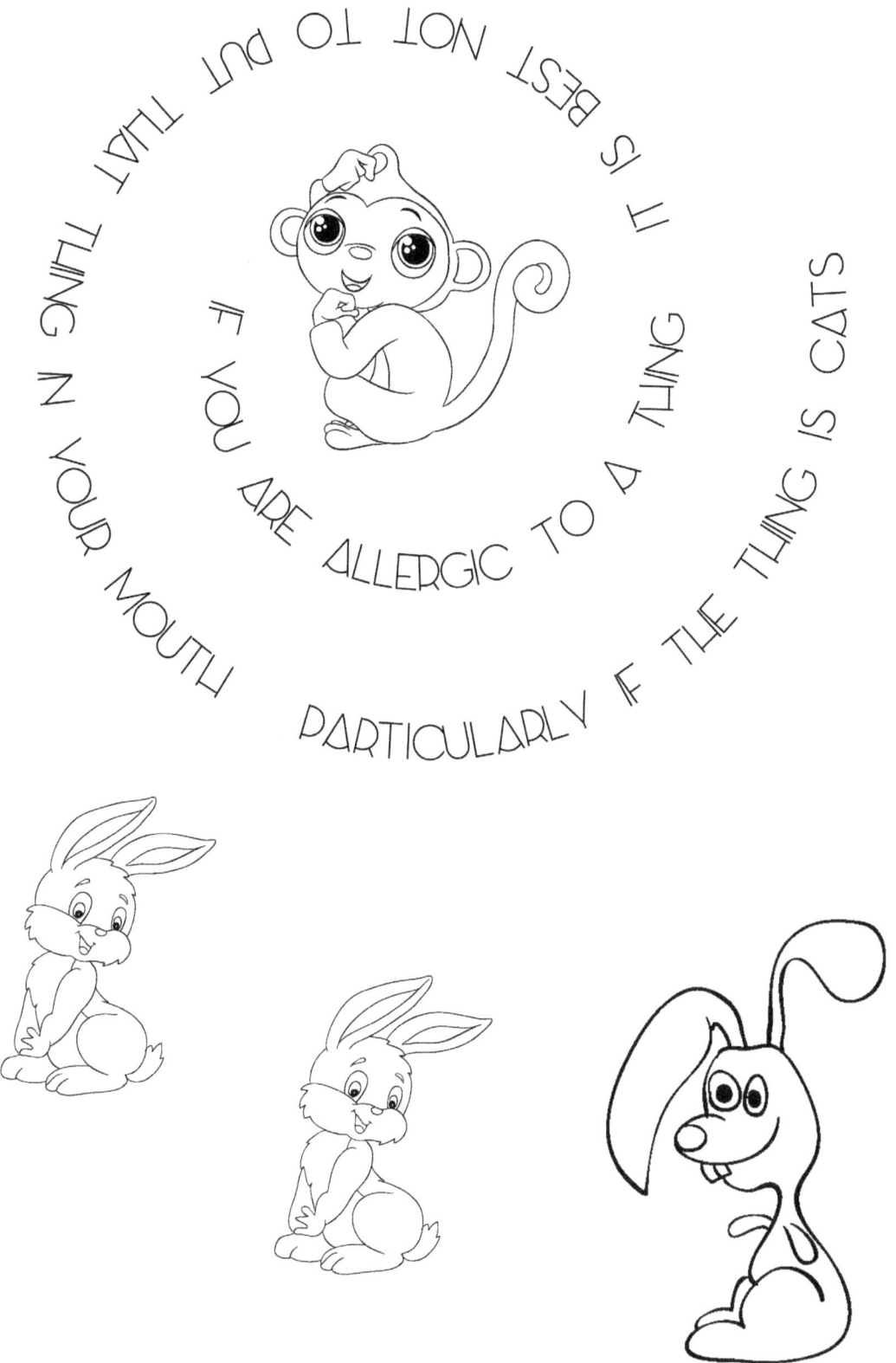

IF YOU ARE ALLERGIC TO A THING IT IS BEST NOT TO PUT THAT THING IN YOUR MOUTH PARTICULARLY IF THE THING IS CATS

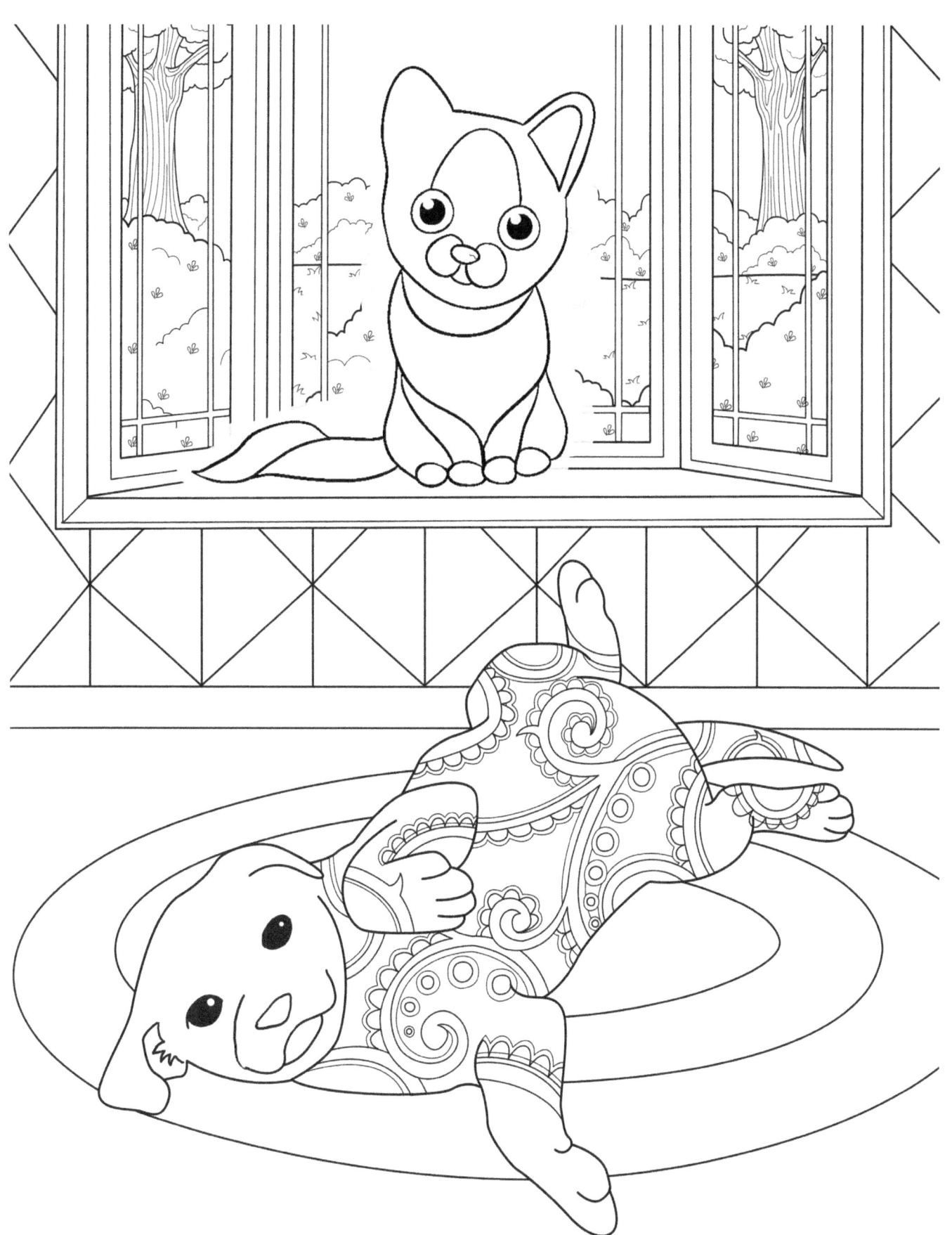

A cat does not want all the world to love her. Only those she has chosen to love.

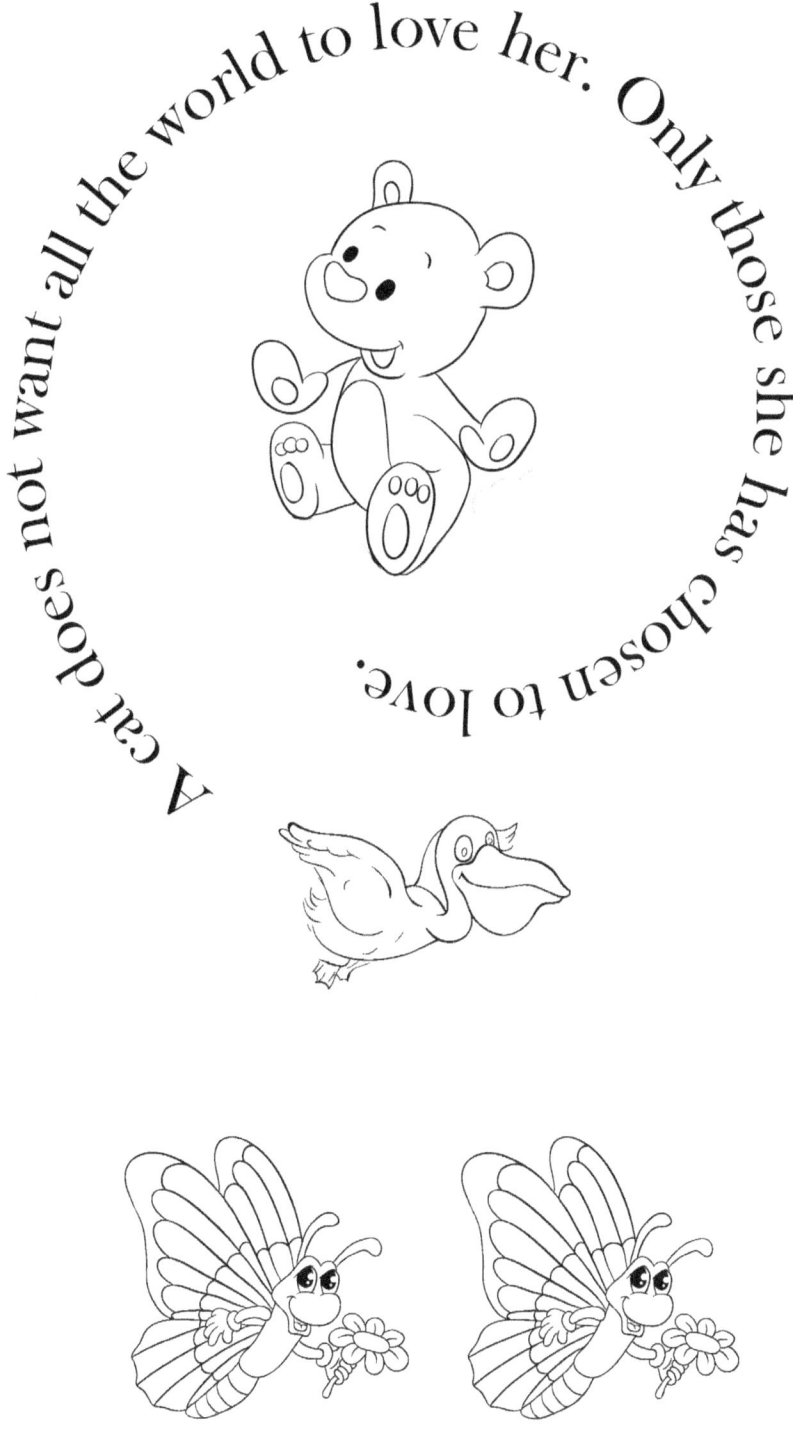

www.ingramcontent.com/pod-product-compliance
Lightning Source LLC
Chambersburg PA
CBHW080629190526
45169CB00009B/3329

* 9 7 8 1 5 3 0 5 6 3 1 0 4 *